Rhyming
My Religious
Thoughts

To Help Make Sense of the Sacred.

By: oldbuck

II

DEDICATION

To all of them:
I want to say thank you for what you just did.
Your reading this book makes me feel like a kid.

You'll soon find I'm no poet, they mostly just rhyme.
Thing's needn't be perfect all of the time.

I don't ask for much money or rich's or fame,
I just like to "make" fun 'cause life's a long game.

So if as you read this you get a big grin,
You laugh or you giggle I'll feel I did win.

For that's the real goal of the time I invest,
A world filled with laughter is the aim of my quest.

So Thanks once again for filling my needs.
It's folks just like you for which my heart bleeds.

~~~~~~

A special note to folks that will find errors.

I apologize in advance for my obvious ignorance.
When they went over punctuation, capitalization
grammar, and spelling in grade school:
This old rhyming fool,
Deserved a "dunce" shaming stool.
'Cause he always made clowning the rule
Instead of listening, way back in grade school.
Think of it as just part of my writing style.
Maybe like an amateur Samuel Clemens. :o)
Thank you. Oldbuck

ACKNOWLEDGMENTS

For all their help on this little book of rhymes, some of it going back many years, I am deeply grateful to the following groups and individuals.

- My family for supporting my rhyming in so many different ways.

- For my Savior Jesus Christ. Who's ministry and finished work have been an often reoccurring theme of my writing from the start.

- For the Holy Spirit's support and encouragement when others weren't able to be there.

- To Calvary Church friends, some have been a sounding board for me a bit over 50 years.

- For all the hundreds of folks that have received pesky emails with lengthy rhymes attached without blocking my name or sending me SPAM.

- To Clement Clarke Moore and his "Twas the Night Before Christmas" for showing me as a small boy, poetry & rhyming could be just for fun.

- To Create Space that made the publishing easier than I ever imagined it could be.

CONTENTS

I trust you grabbed some snacks.

You may not want to put this down
until you've finished.

I wouldn't want it to be a cause
of hunger for anything
but Christ.

ONE OF LIFE'S TREASURES

I have something whose "cash" value is of little concern
But its value to me is growing, this is something I learn.

I have a neat treasure. Tiffany is the name.
The halo 'round her face like pure gold, all the same.

The day that we met all wrapped in light blue
With long flowing ribbons the very same hue.

When we first came together I proudly showed her to friends.
Now when they greet us they may think there's no end.

When I turn to her with a questioning look.
She's seldom ever wrong. Reads my mind like a book.

She's so full of energy her hands never stop,
I'm so proud of her my shirt buttons may pop.

We'd been together but a very short time.
I add a gold band. She looks really fine.

But we do part at bedtime it wouldn't be right.
Her face on my pillow by my side through the night.

There's no guarantee how long this will last,
I'm just hoping the future is as good as the past.

The way things are looking we're both in good shape
Maybe we'll go out together in a box that's flag draped.

Now I thank my employer for giving to me.
This neat little watch. The brand ?..... Tiffany.

Written by oldbuck about the 25 yr. watch he received from his employer. The rhyme was written for and read at, an Adult Bible Class Christmas party. Each one had been asked to be prepared to share something about themselves others might not know. This would be the start of my rhyming phase in 2006. 'o)

The Old Man In The Mirror.

I'm standing here now all ready to shave.
Thinking life's almost over so what have I gave?

Have I cared about others outside of my greed?
Have I ever been generous to those in real need?

I've made a good living though I'm not really rich.
I'll probably leave some to be pitched in a ditch,

By those that had watched me, so often found fault
Bet it won't be enough that they'll need a big vault.

My plan at the end is to bounce the last check,
For the funeral, a casket, and flowers what the heck,

They make lots of money playin' on feelings,
This time they might be left just empty peelings.

I've tried a good life though often I've faltered.
I'm oft driven by others as though I were haltered.

I can't always say that it's been lots of fun.
We can't always help the things that we've done,

They say that God knows way down in his Soul,
I'm more than just simply a grumpy old troll.

He knows of the good things I've wanted to do
But sometimes the money or time they just flew.

Weren't always there at all when I should've
Or help a lot more I very well could've.

Well don't weep for me; I've done what I've done
There's no one to blame, no I'm just the one.

They say that we do what we really want too
I hope in my case that wasn't all true.

For I know of sometimes I wanted to help
But just couldn't stand the yip and the yelp

Of those all around me that often said "No"
We can use those resources to put on our show.

We can buy a new car or a pair of high boots
We can buy a big steak or a closet of suits.

We may need "things", don't throw cash around
Tomorrow might find us asleep on the ground.

You never know when times could get tough
You may lose your job and things would be rough.

So you sock it away for "some rainy day"
Live your whole life in this "too careful" way.

You check every month for the very best rate,
Worry musty CD's won't mature the right date.

That day always comes too soon in the end,
You find you still hoard, some money could spend,

You lie in the box and look all around,
There's nary a pocket or purse to be found.

To store all that stuff at times seemed so precious,
Later they'll serve steaks, grilled rare & delicious.

They'll very soon forget this old man in the mirror,
Someone will come and be nearer and dearer.

Written by oldbuck, after shaving.
They say in the end, when you pull your wet hand
from a bucket of water it doesn't leave a hole very long. I believe it.
But I have known a few that left the water warmer, longer.

Don't Write It On Their Epitaph.

When I was but a little tyke
A phrase I'd heard grown-ups relate.
"Don't write it on their epitaph"
"Don't spend kind words too late".

Others passing will seldom notice
Kind words now spent 'bout others.
Would have meant so much more
If shared by friends or brothers.

Why is it hard to find the phrase
That says the things we aim to say?
Harder still to find a time
To share kind words amidst the fray.

Today your name has crossed my path
Reminded me of times gone by.
Times of joy, or fear, or triumph
Each time we part with but: "Good bye."

Well I had "time" today to set a spell.
To stop and pause and gather thoughts.
Now I'll share what's on my mind
How knowing you much goodness brought.

We all know folks, nice people too
The type we all call: "Kind and Just"
But few we know are always there
When good times turn to bitter "rust.

That few that always seem to care
Have that sense of "What's happened there".
Will always take the time to stop
To sit and listen when ya need to share.

Well you know by now I'm meaning you
We've known each other for "Oh so long".
But in those years I've never said:
"Thanks for being so near and strong."

So I'll "not" write these here kind thoughts
Upon you tomb or graveside rock.
I'll write them here for YOU to read
Each time you have an "elder" block. 'o)

As you think back to what you've done
Take out this rhyme and read anew.
How much you friendship meant to me
My care for you just grew & grew.

Written by oldbuck, as he thought about some of the wonderful folks he's
known through the years and how seldom
we tell them how much their friendship has meant.

That oldbuck's epitaph might read:
"OH THAT I LIVED, THAT A THOUGHT OF ME, MIGHT WARM THE MEMORIES OF THOSE I LEFT BEHIND."

Sample of an old Epitaph;

"Stop ye travelers as you pass by
As you are now, so once was I
As I am now, soon you shall be -
Prepare yourself to follow me."
* * * * *
"But too follow me, don't be content --
How do you know, which way I went?"
* * * * *
And as you think upon that thought,
Was I called or was I sent?

An Easter "Eve" reminder:

The 'Clock of Life' is wound but once
No man has the power to tell
Just when the hands will stop or what may ring his bell.

Now is the only time you own. Live, love, and toil with will.
Place no faith in life or time. For both may soon be still.

For only He can know for sure what is in store for you.
A longer life with gold and jewels or short with rewards few.

It's best we're kept not knowing, we'd worry needlessly
It's best we only trust in Him, for trusting is the key.

So brace yourself and buckle in as life may seem so wrong
Remember this for sure is true. He's with you all along.

For life is just a test at best. He aims to prove your will.
He deserves to know your mind. For He has paid your bill.

This brings us now to Easter Day
Tomorrow won't come late.
He died for us but lives again, that's what we'll celebrate.

So when you're tucking in tonight take some time to pray,
Thank you Lord, In Jesus name. Is all you need to say.

Written by oldbuck

This Easter time poem was prompted by one
written on a scrap of paper they say was found
in a dead man's pocket.
Author unknown

RHYME 5

This is a "poetic" reminder of what some old souls mind may be going through today. It's included here to remind you to stop by and brighten an elderly friend's day this week.

Easter is past....I look out my window to the future:

Tis a still Easter eve and all through my home
Not a creature is stirring; it's just me . . . all alone.
I'll be up all night to shuffle here and there
Or maybe soon I'll be asleep in my chair.

I look ahead to morning when Easter has passed
I'm all bundled up and the blower is gassed.
I'm up and at it, shaved and dressed.
But look, there's no snow. I'm so very depressed.

I've had my oatmeal and toast with no jam
I'd just as soon had fried eggs and some ham.
That's bad for you or so they say
What will I do the rest of today?

These retirement years can seem so long
Some exercise daily to stay fresh and strong
We all rise too early and stay up too late.
I wonder why for we have no real date.

I have a few friends that smile all the time
They simply refuse to pout or to whine
They put up a good front; make it look like it's fun
But there are few I'd leave alone with rope or a gun.

I don't mean to be morbid or gloomy
I just see them as patients without any roomies,
Their days often spent with Drs and such
That really can't help the pain very much.

7

No real good reason to drag this thing out
No place to go or young folks about
How are we doing? Or what's our luck?
Our kids are so busy just making a buck.

They all have their partners and kids that do matter
They already have far too much on their platter.
To bother with us, for we'd just ramble on
If they did stop by or use a "cell" on the run.

I've noticed these changes as I've left my job
I'm stiff and sore; my head's starting to bob
I can't climb many stairs or walk very far
Don't see well enough to still drive my car.

These Golden years are not for faint hearted
At age 69 your troubles just started,
Those checks coming in are welcome of course
But check out my wheels, they're not on a Porsche.

I've money enough if I don't last too long
I'd go to a home but if my decision is wrong
And I run out of cash before I can leave
I'd sit day by day to fear and to grieve.

"Well you've gone on long enough"
Some say in a tone that's really quite gruff.
"No one cares to hear all your chatter"
"Cause in the end it don't really matter."

I do have a small wish; I'd beg you to keep
It costs you nothing, it really is cheap.
Just remember me as a goofy old fox
Way after I've gone in the tightly sealed box.

Written by oldbuck, as he thought of some of the elderly
he had visited the last few days.

Good Times Don't Just Happen

As always with Baptists. There's lots of good food.
It's part of the magic. Get's folks in the mood.
We say: "We're old friends". But don't get together.
Unless there is food and near perfect weather.

And then what you plan can make it or break it.
We wish for variety but can't really take it.
So it comes down to this, if we're to be friends.
It takes lots of food and drinks till the end.

I'd like to here say it's not really that way.
But try it sometime most folks seldom stay.
If games and chit chat is all that there is.
We'd need be good friends or golly, gee, whizzzz.

I can see you out shopping or oft in church halls.
If bouncing hot gossip off of the walls.
Is all that we need to bond us as friends.
Our relations won't last. Will soon reach its end.

It's better to meet and toast a hot pie.
We remember those things till the day that we die.
That time spent together around a potluck.
Means a lot to most folks, even "frumpy" oldbuck.

The fires still hot for toasting marshmallows.
All had a few smores down to the last fellow.
Well it's over now, the mess is picked up.
That last roasted hot dog has now been chewed up.

The tables are moved back where they belong.
It takes four good folks, each one must be strong.

Those tables made of planks. They built them to last.
Pranksters can't run with them very fast.

Folks have said their good-byes and have driven away.
The parties now over there's not much to say.
It was a great time. Took lots of good planning.
From providing the foods, Hey ! the embers need fanning.

The folks that we had assigned to the task.
Seem willing to work but are too often asked.
Some are willing to do. Some are willing to let'em.
But that's part of church work, it don't seem to fret'em.

It all started by 5 and it's now nearly 10.
We had so much fun let's do it again.
"Thank you" never seems like quite enough said.
But any more praise might go to their head.

So, I'll end it here smeared ink have I laid.
Thank you folks much till you're better paid.

Written by oldbuck, as he wrote
a sincere thank you to those that had worked so
hard at the social.

I included this one as a reminder to all of us
There are folks in our churches that work year in and year out
with little or no recognition. Maybe you could search out one of
those folks and let them know how much you appreciate
all that they do.

If you are one of those folks. . . . .
Thank you.

We Study, a Library of Books.

I meet once a week with a group of my peers.
We meet together, we share laughter and tears.
During these sessions we pull out our Book.
Our one constant aim is to give a hard look.

At this "library" of books we call our "Holy Bible".
To call less than Holy would make us feel libel.
My saying: Library, may seem like a trick.
But counting the books we now find sixty-six.

We've been meeting together, some for over forty years.
You'd think after that long it's packed between my ears.
But I sadly must say each time we are tested.
There are always so many by which I am "bested".

Well this current project will go for 12 weeks.
In that length of time we'll take more than a peek.
We started right out just one month ago.
We covered and sorted and didn't go slow.

It was the entire Old Testament in less than one hour.
The teacher did a great job, it tested lungs power.
That's a report to the class of the first thirty-six.
Too tell in short order to give us a fix.

Of how all those books and the words they contain.
All fit together when we cover them again.
The second week was similar, lead by a fearless leader.
He made the New Testament a good solid feeder.

For the weeks that lay ahead we'll be given 10 keys.
To the secrets of these books, it sounds like I tease.

But then came week three and a video we viewed.
This great little speaker preached and reviewed.

How all this got started, the Book and its story.
It started out great but ended "sorta gory".
You see, this young couple were given quite a lot.
But now eating from an apple put them on the spot.

God had plainly spoken, His words, foretold their end.
He had said:" If you do that". "From this place I'll surely send."
So as session three ended our naked little duo.
Were sent now out the gate, it sounded Oh, so cruel.

Since then I have seen a picture once used.
To depict that rare moment, a horrible view.
It shows the young couple, just how they must feel.
Lead from this garden, the gate forever sealed.

As they gaze at sins serpent that tempted this grief.
Nearly tripping on brambles that lay at their feet.
A great fiery sword now swings back and forth.
As the angel now leading offers them no support.

But there's yet more in store for them and for us.
The details of their fall may cause us to blush.
For as the story unfolds we judge them now guilty.
But the Book says of us we are equally filthy.

But I get ahead of myself, we go to week four.
The Short list of rules are laid out before.
They seem easy enough, we first read them through.
No real reason for worry. No big hullabaloo.

I can follow direction; I can go where He leads.
But something soon tells me it ain't just as it reads.
We look thru the Book and find written there.
There are some fine lines, as fine as frog's hair.

To murder it seems is just making a wish.
Covet it said: Is wanting a friend's new satellite dish.
I won't go into adultery, I don't mean to discuss.
Now is seems that it's easy. But could raise quite a fuss.

For just taking a look at some sweet little chick.
Could send you just flying up that "proverbial" crick.
Well I've gone on too long, that's par for the course.
I always take off like I'm on a fresh horse.

I think that the finding for me here today.
The laws were not written in a hard or mean way.
I hear now a voice not booming or harsh.
More like the evening mist across a sweet marsh.

It's filled with desire for me to surrender.
To let the rules lead me, be no longer an offender.
But one of His own. It sounds like He's saying
If I'd give up trying and just get down to praying.

It seems God is here saying if I rightly understood.
These rules should be easy, if each day I now would.
Turn the reins to the Spirit. Let him have control.
He'll take me right home and into God's fold.

But I'll sum it all up what I seem to see.
This Book grows in "value" whatever that be.
And the story we find here will be one of great love.
It's all been made possible. He came down from above.

Too fill in for us, to now take our place.
To offer His Father our now righteous face.

Written by oldbuck,
after returning from Adult Bible Class.

Look closely at the Book,
His truth is found there.

I'm sitting here now and looking way back.
I soon realize how demons attack.
I grew up truth knowing. I oft went to church.
I heard of Salvation for what that's really worth.

As a young lad I went every week,
One night to see a wet girl, to take a quick peek.
That didn't work out they baptized full dressed.
I'd wasted an evening, felt a little depressed.

There wasn't a lot for a young man to do.
But pranks and mischief were more than a few?
But no real bad "sin" for a good guy like me.
I was turning out great; it was so plain to see.

Well the years flew by, I got really serious.
I taught Bible classes, excited near delirious.
Married and three kids, we took them each week.
As our kids grew up, their hearts pure to keep.

Closer to Jesus, Was the life plan.
We wanted them raised His biggest fans.
This went on for years through life's joys and tears
For half of a century I've had no real fears.

I had always just thought that I was real strong.
Able to handle all that went wrong.
Oh there were times; I'd drop to my knees.
I guess I thought praying met one of mans needs.

For it couldn't be easy getting in through that gate.
My habits were good but not really that great.
The day quickly came, they closed that dark lid.
From their grinning faces my own was now hid.

I can't tell the time in minutes or days,
But I soon found myself almost in a haze.
I'm sitting upright in a white colored gown.
I assume I'm in line for heaven I'm bound.

I look all around and folks that I knew.
I'd never have guessed they'd be going there too.
There were men of bad rep. And gals dressed in punk,
There was one guy I knew, never more than a drunk.

And others I saw you can tell by their looks.
He won't find their names when he checks his books.
It's my turn to speak, they seem to ask questions.
I'll know all the answers. I'd taught all those lessons.

He says: "What's your name?" I'm afraid I felt silly.
He don't know my name. I'll tell him it's Billy.
I try to be cute; I could tell he's not buying.
For only my good, this fellow's just trying.

To find a real name to put with this sinner.
If I want to get in, in time for the dinner.
It's a banquet he says, it's on every night.
I quickly apologize, I don't want a fight.

I sincerely reply. It's under oldbuck.
He checks that out. He's having no luck.
He looks up again, and says: "Try another"
That name's not found here for you or a brother.

I told him my story, all the good and the bad.
But shared no decision, which made him look sad.

He said:" You don't get it; it's not about livin'"
"It's not about church goin' or generous givin'."

"It's about your decision. Did you make it or not?
Jesus Name is the way that you get past this spot."
I don't know how this ended for I woke with a start,
I had dreamed of a guy who'd not been very smart.

But he's still got some time to make the right choice
That great Holy Spirit will hear his weak voice.
Write his name down in that book bright and fair.
So he won't be wanting when he finds himself there.

I think I learned something in the dark of that night.
You can't be good enough, you're not always right.
I've settled with Him. I've promised to try.
To follow Him daily. Till that day that I die.

His promise to me, He'll always be near.
Through good times and bad I've nothing to fear.
I understand now the book they go through
It's not a long list of the things that you do.

It's simply a record, a name written down,
The moment you make that great turn around.
You make Him your King. Let Him rule your life.
That simple act removes all of life's strife.

I didn't say sweet roses will litter your path.
I hope you don't think you'd get a free pass.
He still wants your life to be a good sample,
To point others to Him by a Christian example.

Written by oldbuck, as he thought
about his own story and would he
have courage to "rhyme that"?

16

Mirror Never Calls My Name.

Snow White's evil stepmother had a great mirror.
She'd ask it a question but once to her horror.
It gave not her name, instead said another.
This greatly tormented this evil stepmother.

Well years have gone by and now that I'm older
I remember that tale but I've gotten much bolder.
Each morning I stand and look into the glass.
I'm hoping here now to let some time pass.

I can't look much worse, my eyes slowly open.
My wrinkles may fade; At least that's my hopin'
I'm long past my prime I understand that.
Fast approaching the end is about where I'm at.

I'm sure I'm not first to give it some thought.
How I spent my life, just what has it bought?
What do folks that I know think of oldbuck.
I'll ask this old mirror and hope for some luck.

Old mirror of mine just tell me the name.
I'd like to know now who's best played the game.
Some one that's most honest, I'd like to hear from.
He made a good living; He's not just a bum.

Mirror steams over, I hear her wheels spinning.
She soon has a name, Says: "This fellows winning."
Archie's the name. I know the man well.
I can't doubt the mirror that answer is swell.

Thousands of times in all the years past.
His generous portions built a business to last.

He's worked long & hard but now has a grand kid.
To chase deer and raccoons, to try to get rid.
Of all those outsiders that come to small farms.
If you don't stay on them, they do you great harm.

Days may grow to weeks before courage I get.
To ask her again But I'll soon do it, I bet.

Mirror I'm looking for some generous person.
Who's given to all when times were a worsenin'
She says since the flood, there have been oh so many.
But one name stands out; He'd give his last penny.

But money's not all this one will give out.
He gives of his time with never a pout.
Old Bernie's the name she lays now on me.
I have to admit, none better would be.

I've known him nearly all of my life.
He and Loretta, His loving wife.
I couldn't tell you the hundreds of times.
He stopped what he's doing and turned on a dime.

To come to my aid whatever the need.
That man is so generous. He doesn't know greed.
Well, this makes it harder to ask the next time.
A listing of "character" I'd wish left behind.

To put with my name to reflect what I've done.
There's one more I'll ask and that's the last one.
Oh mirror of mine I've one last request.
I don't ask it lightly or even in jest.

There must be someone among all your travels.
That you count as bravest, with courage of gravel.
Well that's a big order, this countries at war.
There are thousands out there, will be thousands more.

18

Willing to die for family and friends.
That daily will face very uncertain ends.
But you want a name; I'll give you one now.
You may even wonder, you picked him just how?

Well courage is something that's hard to describe.
Some charge the front line, some turn down a bribe.
Some carry big weapons, some sneak in the night.
But there's one form of courage I think is so right.

The courage to face whatever he must.
Sickness or hardship or finances a bust.
Well there's one you know when I say his name.
You'll soon understand. I'm playing no game.

Harold it is. He's faced more than most.
Yet he still stands like a sturdy steel post.
He's had many hardships and never complains.
And if any good happens he's the first to exclaim.

Mirror you're right. He's a man of true grit.
I'd not measure up, I wouldn't be fit.
To walk in his shoes not even one day.
He's been a good friend all of the way.

Well, I'd better examine my life even better.
She's had these guys pegged right down to the letter.
There's one thing I've done, it may save my soul.
It's something that surely has taken no toll.

Maybe that's why it scares me to think it will work.
To say just a Name now seems like a quirk.
But I've checked it out, I've read through the Book.
I've gone more than once to take a hard look.

But it's written there. "Believe on His Name".
And when you get there He'll cover your shame.
Again someone else is taking my place.
Helping me out, get's me now through the race.

I've shown no real drive to help other folks.
I've been more a stooge, a teller of jokes.
I hope my lucks better when I near that gate.
This filthy looser, Gatekeeper won't hate.

I trust His promise, my name written there.
I'll probably get in by the breadth of a hair.
If you've reached that point, you've talked to your mirror,
As you look around. There's so many that's dearer.

You may find yourself in a similar spot.
You'll want to go there, not where it's so hot.
So today is the day. Get right with the Lord.
He'll forgive your sins and let you on board.

Dig out that dusty Bible. Read it day by day.
It will plainly show you what Jesus has to say.
Then get to work. Share Christ with a friend.
For if He's in your heart 'twill be your life's trend.

Written by oldbuck, after a morning sermon on
Folks being famous. Our long time friend "Harold" has since
passed away. Of course all these names have been changed
to protect their privacy.

"Pride indeed is the cardinal vice -- it swings open the door to most of the other
theological vices, and undermines the classical virtues of prudence, courage and
justice. It thrives, not on what one has, but on what others do not have. And even
when one has diligently practiced the most admirable virtues, there always lurks
the danger that at some moment one will look in the mirror and say: 'Oh my! What
a wonderful person I am!' Thus does the vice lunge from its hiding place."
Author unknown

Colossians 2:18B
Mans unspiritual mind puffs his head
Full of idle notions. Paraphrased

We hold fast to idle idols

Idle is one of those words you must know the spelling.
To rightly get hold of the story it's telling.
For being idle is what granite rocks do.
As they sit around just waiting for you.

To skip them on water or be a pet in your pocket.
They're "hard" to beat, you can't really knock it.
You can crush them all up to spread on your drive.
Or polish and carve for a friend, no longer alive.

In all of these cases the rock does the same.
They just lay around; it's all the rocks game.
With some, the word Idle oft brings lots of frowns.
You ought to be busy not just lying around.

But there's another idol. The kind we keep quiet.
We'd just as soon others didn't know that we buy it.
It's those scary things we find in our lives.
That grab our attention, least a wink of our eye.

It could seem a small thing, the idol we seek.
We don't really linger, we planned to just peek.
Sure we invest money but what doesn't cost.
Without some investment most fun would be lost.

An idol may exist in the eye of the beholder.
Not something we own like a thick CD folder.
Material things can't be all that bad.
We're taught to be frugal by our mom and dad.

So let's think about this. Great "idol" star winners,
That sing and perform, may appear to be sinners.
Some word's they use, some clothes they wear
Tattoos and piercings, have I mentioned their hair?

May seem out of place in a "self-righteous" church.
But not seeing them there should even be worse.
Does it mean we tell them they are not welcome here?
We need to remember the devil is near.

If we can't shed our idols should they look to us?
What an example we set to gain love and trust?
I guess what I'm saying but not very well.
Is our living example steering someone toward hell?

So look all around what is it you hold?
Above everything else it could never be sold.
Its tops on your list of life's little treasures.
It's the best of your life by all of your measures.

If your single great treasure, it's not Jesus you await,
You'll find yourself wanting when you get to that gate.
For God says it plainly, He don't stammer or stutter.
The Almighty is first or you end in the gutter.

Well, I've gone on too long, I started this out.
With scripture for warning what I'd be talkin' about.
For my kind of idle leaves my mind wide open.
It fills up with garbage, at times needs a soapin'.

I close with the light I've seen in the distance.
I know I have Jesus. I'll show no resistance.
When He comes again for His very own,
I'll be packed and ready to go right on home.

Written by oldbuck, after returning home
from a great worship service that included
a thought provoking message on Idols.

What Could We Be Doing?

For quite some time I've pondered and thought.
Asked many folks and this is the story it brought.
My concern is for folks that oft' come around.
But then for some time are nowhere to be found.

What is current practice? What is it we do?
So when they are missing they don't drop from view.
They say: "In small groups" We all can keep track.
But if they're not in one, they may fall through a crack.

We all seemed to agree it might be a weak link.
But what to do next would take some deep think.
What did the church do? When I first belonged.
That made it grow to a "body" so strong.

There was a different feel back there in the past.
Maybe things were slower didn't move along so fast.
Folks oft stopped to visit on their way out of church.
Long lines at the restaurants didn't drive us to lurch.

Most ate at their homes, took a nap, then got ready.
Sunday night was a big deal as trumpets blew steady.
We'd sing and we'd pray and when it was time.
We'd all match up; at a friend's home to dine.

Those lunches however seemed to get out of hand.
Some got so fancy; they'd nearly hire a band.
To get to know each other as we did way back then.
We now email or text or it's time on the internet we spend.

It's part of our culture, we've drifted apart.
I'm missing the contact; it's left a hole in my heart.

But wait just a minute, I've wandered away.
From my original topic. The Lord's work for today.

As I now think on it, we live in the age,
When computers and info are all of the rage.
Is there a way? To make technology work.
To aid in a church, to make it a new "perk".

Most now have email and a big excel sheet.
Could we start up files? Too know when folks meet?
Suppose every family were given 5 names.
Folks they would follow. Sort of make it a game.

Each would keep track on their own excel sheet.
Of those on their list they happened to meet.
Or what if they didn't see a face on their list.
They could send'em an email; tell them they're missed.

The aim of this all isn't to catch someone napping.
A friend who was missing. To make them feel sappy.
But to just keep in touch in an age that's so shattered.
To let someone know their missing has mattered.

We all need someone at one time or another.
To just say:" I missed ya". It needn't be to bother.
Well as has been my life's practice, I've gone on and on.
Like so many "ideas" "It's easier said than it's done."

Written by oldbuck after pondering what his church
family might do to encourage missing church folks.

This rhyme was included to prompt each one that reads it to consider: What
am I doing in my church to let folks know "I missed them?"

A Christmas Time rhyme.

I sit now at the keyboard
With Christmas on my mind.
I had planned a Christmas letter
But a short rhyme might be fine.

As I've thought about last year
Most of us have had our share
Of days with sadness, days with cheer.
Some with laughs, some with care.

But as we come to this fine time
Our hearts are filled with joy.
Of Christmas gifts and giving
A tie, some sweets, our kids a toy.

So I've decided to skip the news
Of my grandkids and neighbors pets.
And in this space remind again
Of God's FREE gift and what man gets.

What a humble start in stables air
Asleep in a manger, quiet & still.
The Christ child lies as but a babe
To bring for us, his blood to spill.

That this young "King" we now take note
Had started out as no one had.
And finished as The King above
To make believers, forever glad.

So as you raise your song or cup
At this fine Season of the year.
Keep always there within your heart
Your Christ is now and ever near.

Remember now and years to come
As days will come for lots more fun.
The Reason for the Season
His work has really just begun.

oldbuck

All my life, Christmas has held a very special place in our family and many families across America. It seems to be getting more and more crowded out now by "Frantic Merchants" desire to "get their share" of American's lust for more stuff.
I would ask each one that reads this to pause and consider the real

REASON FOR THE SEASON

To those of other Faiths, I pray God's continued Grace & Mercy, not only during the Christmas Season but all through the coming New Year.

How a Young Boy, Defeated a Giant.

A long time ago in a land far, far away.
Some trouble was stirring, but why? We can't say.
An evil, enemy's army entered Israel's land.
With horses and chariots and a huge fighting band.

They soon pitched their tents on a mountain top near.
Where Saul and his army could see and might fear.
But the fight didn't start like most fighting did.
It seems that some secret . . . this enemy's hid.

They sent just one soldier, a giant, not a man.
He challenged Saul's army to fight hand to hand.
Send out your best, we'll fight till one bends.
Whichever one wins. Brings this war to an end.

Well a giant is huge, like four normal men.
Who would go out? Which man can we send?
The Israelite army shaken was moved from their mark.
They trembled and shook each night after dark.

For early each morning as the sun was coming up.
Goliath was out there, they whimpered like pups.
About this same time on another hill side.
Young David was watching dad's sheep with great pride.

For just a day earlier a lion had come near.
And grabbed a young lamb, David sprang with no fear.
He chased down the lion and grabbing a hold.
Lion dropped the scared lamb; He raced back to his fold.

But David held on, the lion grew madder.
And thought of the lunch he'd so nearly had'er.

27

But David held on to the lion's great head.
When the fight ended the great lion was dead.

Just a few days before a bear had come round.
He felt also a lamb for his lunch he had found.
As was shepherd's duty he had chased the bear down.
And when it was over, bear's dead on the ground.

But why bring this shepherd into this "giant" tale.
David had three brothers, in the army, growing pale.
Jesse their father and young David's too.
Feared for his son's, didn't know what to do.

He packed some parched corn and ten loaves of bread.
Told young David to go "See your brothers well fed."
"Here's some cheese for their brave army friends."
"Find out while you're there, is the war near its end?"

For this fearless young shepherd an adventure was in store.
He'd soon see the army and so very much more.
The sun was barely shining when David got to camp.
Soldiers just getting up. Morning dew was still damp.

Everyone was facing across the green valley.
Counting enemy soldiers to get a clear tally.
But what caught their eye was that "mountain of brass".
Coming their way, approaching real fast.

It was Goliath the giant. All dressed in full armor.
On his head a brass helmet, there's no way to harm'er.
He's shouting his boast as he had forty times.
David now is wondering if giant hadn't crossed the line.

Why do we stand here? With God on our side.
Why tremble in fear, some run to now hide.
I'll go with God's strength and bring him on down.
Israel's army must have thought young David's a clown.

When word of this lad came to King Saul.
He wanted to see him, lamb skins and all.
Young David stepped up. He told the king of past days.
How he protected the sheep in so many brave ways.

Defeating vicious hunters with God's mighty hand.
He will do now the same with this threat to Saul's land.
This giant that speaks mockingly of God's chosen few.
"The Lord" will bring down without much "to-do".

This king wasn't sure what this shepherd would dare.
But he knew this great courage among men was so rare.
He took off his great armor; Put it on the young lad.
His helmet and sword, all the helps that he had.

But the sheer weight of it all made David feel bad.
To rely on such stuff might make his God sad.
David said to King Saul, "I can feel in my bones."
"I don't need all this stuff just a hand full of stones."

I'll wear my own clothes as plain as they are.
I'll carry my staff; I'm not going that far.
I've my stones in a sack, my sling in my hand.
My God will today drive these men from His land.

When Goliath saw him coming, this strapping young youth.
It made him so angry for he knew not the truth.
He thought that King Saul was just playing along.
Sending out a young boy, to fight him, was wrong.

But he'd kill all the same, for at the day's end.
Israel would be slaves, No courage to defend.
The giant shouted out, "I'll rip you to shreds.
The birds will then eat you like crumbs of dry bread".

David quickly replied: "You have only your sword."
"But I have the power and strength of my Lord."

29

With that the young servant charged straight at his foe.
And with his small sling a stone he would throw.

Right square in the forehead, it stunned the great beast.
He fell to the ground. . . . The giant is now least.
As our story now ends, Philistines on the run.
God's faithful servant has his day in the sun.
. . . . but that's for next time.

Written by oldbuck,
in response to a friend that wanted him to try writing
a children's Bible story rhyme.

This was included on the outside chance the reader might know of a young
person that might enjoy hearing / reading a wonderful story from the Bible.
I believe it is a True story about Real people and a Real God.

May the Lord lead your thoughts as you consider a young person that might
profit from such a reading.

Noah and the Ark

This is a true story about: A good man and a big boat.
A time way back then when all would need to float.
A long, long time ago just after earth was made.
God looked down on it. Saw what evil plans man laid.

For man had started out with sin just filling up their lives.
Now had passed it on to all the children of their wives.
God saw that sin was growing still, by now was really bad.
Because he'd loved his children so, it made him very sad.

I will destroy them, every one; He can't allow to go for ever
Except for Noah & his sons. This tie with evil men He'll sever.
Noah's true at work & worship. This servant gives me hope
I'll help him build a giant Ark large enough that all may float.

It would be huge for sure. Noah and sons work day & night
Built it strong and sturdy. With God's plan to make it tight.
When finished, it lacked nothing. Two by two, get all on board.
For with a pair of every creature. Twill be a sizable hoard.

Be sure there's food enough for them and for yourselves.
Aim to be real generous stocking those pantry shelves.
For it shall rain, non-stop, forty nights and forty days,
Will flood as raging streams overflowing water ways.

For this is how so quickly I'll erase all former life.
Starting fresh as new without the present strife.
So Noah sent for all to come. Male & female, two by two.
Near endless lines, as numbers grew, surely not a few.

With all loaded, safe on board, God secured the only door,
For within that very week God had said that it would pour.

The ark was being thrown about, by storm winds, side to side,
As the fury daily raged, fearful creatures boxed inside.

They were however safe in God's great loving care,
But still it must have given all aboard the Ark a scare.
As the rain had stopped, the trip still far from over
You couldn't now see grass or luscious fresh green clover.

The water still was deeper than the crest of every hill
With water and more water, Earth's crust, far over-filled.
After months of patient waiting Noah sent forth a Raven
In search of dry ground. Which all their feet were cravin'.

The Raven a poor choice they eat flesh near by the pound.
Lots of dead meat carrion, was all that Raven found.
Then Noah sent a Dove to take a fresh new peek
When it came flying back it had fresh leaves held in its beak.

Noah took that as a sign. A few days the bobbing stopped.
Things were looking up. For a mountain they had topped.
They waited a bit more for things to leaf and sprout.
Then Noah set them free to raise families round about.

Well God didn't leave them to worry or to ponder.
When God might choose to send lightning or loud thunder.
If they were now to stray or turn out less than best.
Would God once again put all mankind to the test?

God made them a promise and sealed it with a sign.
When you see a rainbow you will know it's one of mine.
I will remember always this promise I will keep.
Never again to send a flood. Raging waters, Oh so deep.

It will be forever after a sign of safety and rebirth.
Go and bare your young. Re-populate the earth.
So Noah and his wife, three sons and their wives
Left behind the giant Ark to get on with their new lives.

32

What I got from this true story is God loves us very much.
He seeks the best for all of us and wants to stay in touch.
So pray to Him non-stopping, we lack what we don't ask.
Remember: He's "Creator" God. He's big enough for any task.

Written by oldbuck,
when he decided to make a coloring
book about the story of Noah and
The Flood for his grandkids.

I have included this rhyme for all the young people out there that may feel
the story of Noah & the Ark is just a fable. It is far from it and holds some
beautiful pictures of God's concern for each one of His own and the details
of the plan for them.
Please consider sharing this with some young person.
It might very well be the only Bible Story they will ever read.

An Old Man's Bedtime Prayer

Lord: Now I lay me down to rest.
To get away from this days test.
To rest my head on pillows fluff.
To clear my head of all the stuff.

That comes your way as you get old.
It's part of life that's seldom told.
I hope to get some 10 hrs. sleep.
I'll probly end up counting sheep.

As I look back across my days.
I know I've sinned in many ways.
I'm real sorry.   I've told you that.
To say again just sounds "old hat".

But now I plead for this short break.
To get some rest for bodies sake.
If you "Oh LORD" my wish would grant.
And do for me something I can't.

For I've no strength, my life to take.
Just let me die before I wake.
For my old joints have turned to rust.
I'd just as soon they're back to dust.

Lord: If I'd wake and look about.
I'd "Hoot & Holler" and give a shout.
If I would find that was my fate.
To there be standing inside "The Gate"

To know at last I'd passed the test.
I don't need seats among the best.
It's enough to not be missed.
My name was on His special list.

But you know best I'm sure of that.
So if I wake I'll just hang pat.
I'll dream of red, rare steaks so fat
To ponder where the "Good Times" at.

I'll shuffle through another day.
And burn more bills we strain pay.
To keep us warm in this cold pit.
And by the window now to sit.

As I think back to 'yester' years.
With all the joy, few sprinkled tears.
I never dreamed these "Golden Years"
Would be so filled with pain and fears.

I never thought I'd leave alone.
My wife & I would share our home.
But when I'm gone, alone she'll bow.
She'll need get by . . . I don't know how.

With this I'll close my nightly plea.
I'd be forever in debt to thee.
If you would oft stop by this way.
To comfort wife here every day.

Written by oldbuck, to recognize and honor all the elderly that
struggle with their health, their obligations, their present & their future.

A trip to the Windy City.

I'm planning a trip but not going too far.
It's not like the moon or the nearest bright star.
It's about a 4 hours drive but that's just a guess.
It's been a long time since I've made this same quest.

It's not really a quest; I'm not really in search.
I've just never been to Moody's own church.
I've been to Chicago a long time back.
So long ago, I've sort of lost track.

I was there as a kid, actually lived there a while.
When I try to think back it just brings a weak smile.
I don't think "sad" thoughts, I just can't think at all.
I left as a small boy, only age 6, and not very tall.

As I remember back to my "Blue Island" friends,
I recall its diversity. Where "variety" saw no end.
My dad and his brother built trailer houses small
For vets and young families, home they could call.

But that's not the point, the point is this trip.
I've now sort'a strayed. Once again lost my grip.
Several folks from our church were schooled at Moody.
Located just north of the heart of that Windy City.

But that's part of the trip, to learn what it's like.
The area don't scare us, we won't be taking a hike.
We're going for meetings, the very best kind.
They'll be some of the best, the best Moody could find.

For once every year the school celebrates.
The Founder of course, they feel he should rate.
Some notice, some honor, and they do it up right.
They have strings of great speakers go into each night.

We leave early morning to make the first round.
We'll need grab some grub, a lunch must be found.
Then as meetings will start, it's off to the campus.
We now make choices from those set to pamper us.

There are buses and shuttles to go here and there.
They say it's cold & windy, you're ears can't be bare.
We're told:"Wear several layers and old comfy shoes".
"So as you wait there you won't turn a deep blue."

Well there's not much I can say cause like I've just said.
Its years since I've been there; I've never slept in this bed.
I've not heard these same speakers; nor eaten this food.
I've not even spent time with our little church brood.

But I'm as excited now as I can become.
My wife can confess. Travel for me is seldom welcome.
But there is one thing unique about this short trip.
It's part of an experiment, it's like a flagship.

Since the place we're to go, the meetings we attend.
Are annual events so next year will we send?
Will there be from this group a positive vibe.
Will we on return be able to describe.

Events as they happened in such a positive light.
That others will follow. For reservations, even fight.
For a happening like this can bring something grand.
A kind of 'revival fire' within our small band.

A feeling of warmth may come to our hearts.
A challenge we pickup can be a fresh start.
You can't ever tell what God has in store.
He may very well want our church back for more.

So as I close this rhyme my heads just been whacked.
To pray for the group, the drivers, of course me, as I pack.
That He'll give a safe trip. Lots of keen photo shots.
Open all our minds to a very wide spot.

So when we get back, It's a "thumbs up" that we give.
A new outlook on life, some new way to live.
So next year at this time others that follow.
Will go for a filling won't need to be hollow.

Many years from today as hundreds have gone.
We back at our church will have sung some new songs.

Written by oldbuck,
as he prepared himself for a two
day trip to Founders Week meetings
at Moody Bible Institute, in Chicago.
A school that helps set the world on fire for Christ
student by student.

Other names & places may have been changed to
protect everyone's privacy or reputation. 8^)

I want to thank the folks at Moody for allowing me
To use their "real" name in my book.

RHYME 17

David's Day in the Sun,
"Has Him on the Run".

There's an old Bible story of a young man and his feats.
As part of this long tale a great giant he defeats.
Well what happens then? Just where does that lead?
On to great things or back with lambs to feed.

King Saul can't remember the times in the past.
His mind greatly troubled this lad cleared it up fast.
For he played a lovely harp, sang his great Psalms.
This brought for this King a sense of great calm.

But back to this day, King sent out now a query.
Who was this young man? Not knowing, made him weary.
The Kings right hand man, Abner was his name.
He brought David to Saul to claim now his fame.

Saul said to the lad, "Just who's son are you?"
"Jesse your good servant, we're from Bethlehem too".
Then Saul knew at once this was the same kid.
When David played and sang then from demons Saul was rid.

Someone else comes in play. Jonathan, the Kings own son.
He loved this young friend. Knew they could have some fun.
This would be just the start of a long time friendship.
But wouldn't be complete without some scary hardships.

King Saul made young David, Captain, now of many men.
There must have been at times a thousand strong of them.
They loved their young leader would go anywhere.
Because they saw in his heart Lord God dwelling there.

Soon David was loved, everyone knew he cared.
There's only one that's upset, Saul seemed to despair.
For as with most of us folks, it's fun when we're on top.
But when fame starts to slip it's near impossible to stop.

There was a tune going round. Young ladies oft would sing.
It troubled Saul the King. In his ears the words did ring.
King Saul has slain his thousands, that's always fun to hear.
David's slain ten thousands. That's a little hard to bear.

Another thing was on Saul's mind. Old Samuel had proclaimed:
God would take Saul's kingdom; Perhaps David's now to blame.
As the evil spirits troubled Saul he invited Dave to play.
As he played the sorrow grew Saul's anger raged that day.

His heart grew hard as anger built. He threw a javelin, to kill,
This bright young man before him, with him he'd had his fill.
But now the story's getting grim. Young David stepped aside.
Saul threw the javelin again. Thrones threat just can't abide.

But David's far too quick; Saul's not really a big threat.
But now King Saul is furious. He's not killed this smart kid yet.
Saul makes this soldier an offer that's hard to not here take.
Saul's lovely older princess, David's bride he'll surely make.

Defeat again those Philistines and when you then get back.
She'll be your budding bride, if you survive the last attack.
David is proud to help; it's not just for the bribe.
He'll do anything he can for the King of his own tribe.

This land they both love. These people they serve.
David feels his humble best is the least, from him deserve.
Of course with his God's help David's army wins again.
But the bride he was promised has married some other man.

Saul makes a new deal "Lovely Michal, you love."
"Kill a hundred more Philistines. You and your God above."
"And you'll have her hand, my lovely young princess."
So David runs off quickly. Kills two hundred, not one less.

When he returns Victorious there was a fancy wedding.
But the victories had added to what Saul had been dreading.
This story now turns worse. Saul's wrath only grew.
He called in his servants for advice on: "What to do?"

When his son Jonathan, heard of this terrible plot.
David was his best friend, Kill him, he would not.
So he went to his friend, told him of Saul's plan.
Then went to King Saul to arrange now for a ban.

He reminded the King of all David had done.
Of all the hard battles this brave soldier won.
Had never asked for anything at all from his great King.
Except that one time, the golden wedding ring.

Saul came to his senses, He called off the kill.
David came back home. He thought it was Saul's will.
But back in those times peace didn't last for long.
Someone always wanted to prove they were strong.

So back to the battle, went Captain David and crew.
Then off of those Philistines, their heads and arms flew.
When Saul's army returned to tell The King of the news.
He was furious again at David's rave reviews.

Everyone was ecstatic, this young Captain wins again.
You'd thought by Saul's pout David had done some horrible sin.
David came again to Saul to play a soothing Psalm.
As before it had brought the weary King a great calm.

Saul was so distraught, He took javelin in hand.
With his aim for David to end his time on this land.
David ran home to safety. His wife begged him to leave.
Her dad won't give up; David's surely his pet peeve.

David goes out of town to where Old Samuel abides.
He tells him the tale. Samuel wants him there to hide.
Just stay here with me; you're safe in God's care.
Saul cannot reach you; you're safe from him there.

Soldiers are sent, but won't follow Saul's orders.
To bring David on back across Israel's borders.
Finally Saul comes himself this stray soldier to find.
But soon killing God's friend is far out of his mind.

For when he arrives he sees something unreal.
Samuel, David, and his soldiers, God's presents they now feel.
He bowed down to the earth and worshiped there his God.
David then ran off again for some far off distant sod.

These two aren't here finished, there's far more to these tales.
But we'll see through it all, God's love never fails.
So here's where we end it, this strange Bible story.
At times very loving, at other times real gory.

Written by oldbuck,
This is the fourth in the children's series he's
attempting. That children may learn
of God's great power and love for them.

Back from the Windy City

I'll preface my remarks, I should now keep this quick.
But I'm so full of "Wind" I can't master that trick.
So go back a few days I wrote a travelers rhyme.
Now that I'm back I'll spend a little time.

To tell this true tale of the adventure we took.
Enough great things happened; I could write a short book.
But that's not what I do as by now you all know.
I write silly rhymes and they just seem to grow.

They're not always true, these words I arrange.
This time it's so different, that probably sounds strange.
But you see where we went, is a near Sacred place.
A place where so many "Talk to God" face to face.

Oh I don't mean they've seen him.
They aren't hand-shaking cronies.
But go to Him often. He's expecting no phonies.
I'd better start at the "start" as that often seems best.
Then fill in the blanks with all of the rest.

It's 4:44 now Thursday a.m., it's dark, but wife has been up.
Is now getting ready, but my eyes are shut as a new born pup.
Oh I'm on my feet don't misunderstand.
I'm just not awake, can't give her a hand.

She goes on ahead and gets our stuff ready.
I'm in there shaving, trying now to be steady.
Then in the old van we're now running on time.
We don't want to be late; there might be a big fine.

The bus has pulled up to the door to be loaded.
I've had a big breakfast; I'm a little bit bloated.
But that's not important; As Pastor's packing the bags.
All 16 now are loaded; the bus is starting to sag.

We'll head down the road, With Earl at the wheel.
Pastor Jay will drive later, that's the sensible deal.
For he and wife Donna, both went to school.
At Moody to prepare for "His" worker pool.

Of trained and committed, bright young men and women.
That will join hearts and lives in the fight against sinnin'.
A couple hours down the road we stop for fuel and a break.
Everything takes longer than you think it will take.

We land now at Moody. It's time for some lunch.
As I wait outside the restrooms I spot a face in the bunch.
Yes it's Bart Sampson. A young man I admire.
That stayed once overnight. He's a young man on fire.

He and friend, Duke, share ideas over lunch.
But we need to keep moving for I have a hunch.
This very first speaker will hit the deck runnin'.
His topic is perception and he won't be funnin'.

For he's done lots of study, and has joined with a buddy.
To write now a book, on old church fuddy duddies.
It seems some younger folks hold a lower opinion.
Of today's Christian church and some folks that attend'em.

We're a bit judgmental, Insensitive, hypocritical.
Anti homosexual, sheltered, too focused, and political.
I'm sure that it's true; I feel some of it myself.
When I've said something stupid I've felt "Put on the shelf".

I thought he was grand but had no way of knowing.
The message of speakers would just keep on glowing.
The first evening at church, we wait to get going.
But tension in our group is growing and growing.

It seems one of our ladies has now come up missing.
I get a crazy notion as I hear a near mike hissing.
I could jump to my feet and approach with great fear.
The pulpit at Moody, any pastor would revere.

I could say with all the power that I could surely muster.
"At the end, near the organ""Our group will then cluster".
But it must have been His will that I held my place.
'Cause that would surely have given my wife a red face.

Then our speaker starts to share of the Perfect Storm.
How God's at His best when He sets the norm.
Christian faith has the answer to harsh realities of life.
Christ is essential to overcome today's strife.

The Bible is the place; it's filled with hope and belief.
It's increasingly important we go there for relief.
I won't go into "catching shuttles "It's both funny and sad.
But as it turns out it wasn't really that bad.

Back at our hotel. Up to Room 2044
So many in that room some are sitting on the floor.
There are snacks of all kinds but I'm not eating any.
It's a lovely spread. It cost someone a pretty penny.

It's soon Friday morning, the phone wake-up worked out great.
With free breakfast offered that's even more 'hurry up" bait.
9:30 Another winner speaks of Prophets and cults.
But is very reassuring we'll know truth from what's false.

He listed several identifiers of false teachers and their kind.
So when we hear them talking we will bring those to mind.
If we are to grow and share the Gospel message.
Keep oft in mind; your listeners may live in a dark age.

Our next conference speaker, was a fellow I can't name.
As a speaker holds the floor, this fellow surely will gain fame.
He's a natural speaker but has garnered lots of practice.
He used ample humor but never meant to distract us.

His one simple phrase. I doubt, I'll ever forget.
He spoke of sacrifice, of sharing all you get.
When he finds himself in line, He's breathed out his last breath.
Asked: "What brings you here?"
"I gave my all, then starved to death."

That's just part of what he shared. Forgiveness, love, and giving.
Seem to make so little sense in the days that we're now living.
But those age old acts may play a large and lasting part.
If we're ever going to reach a lost man's broken heart.

Now this sounds deep and sometimes were.
But there's also some silliness thrown in the trips blur.
It's a small sandwich shop a few blocks from campus.
Pastor Jay acts as though he's wanting to feed us.

While we made the trek he gave good directions.
On what to expect of the waiters expectations.
What they'd want to hear, when it's your turn to say.
Be ready with your order or get out of the way.

Well, as is normal, I paid little attention.
So when they got to me they showed little affection.
What do you want? I was asked several times.
I thought I spoke loudly. I at times even mimed.

But too little avail. Those behind me filled them in.
I think the guys working feared I'd never begin.
But I'm not alone wife didn't move her tray.
On down the counter and out of "Spikes" way.

I may have then actually saved my sweet wife.
I moved both trays and they spared her life.
This may seem I didn't like it. Nothings farther from the truth.
It was everything I long for to sooth my "burger tooth".

I laughed and laughed as I stuffed my pudgy face.
We're all from out of town so it didn't disgrace.
Those in our group that tend to hold back.
Would rather be meek than come under attack.

But on our walk back I may have near sealed my fate.
I may have offended a "local", but he showed no real hate.
After lunch I had asked those I felt I might sway,
To take in a speaker we'd already seen by the way.

The second time around was as good as the first.
But it was hard for my wife she was dying of thirst.
A distraction like that can be too much to bear.
When you've heard the guy once the same message to share.

But I found them rewarding. Too soon they were done.
We were back on the bus, this prize was near won.
One last surprise before we reach home.
There's an hour of heavy traffic. Jay's tired to the bone.

But he's a good sport; He's a trick up his sleeve.
We go for some great pizza you'd never believe.
Now it's back on the bus with Earl at the wheel.
He drives all the way back, doesn't seem a big deal.

Well if I were to want to summarize all this.
The back of a greeting card holds this little twist.
It's been said for years will never find rest:
"If you care enough you will give them your best."

I'll say that of those that spoke to the groups.
But also of those in charge of our troops.
What tireless workers, what wonderful sports,
For as we get older we can get out of sorts.

It can be too far to walk. Too cold to stand waiting.
The foods outside my norm. All these crowds can be grating.
This working together, of students short and tall.
To make this week meaningful. Rewarding for all.

Thanks Earl for driving, for all that you did.
Pastor Jay and Donna. You had the energy of kids.
Patience of Job & Solomon's wisdom. Who could ever forget.
The strength of a Sampson, movin' tables in Joliet.

But my favorite player, our teams steady mascot.
Was our "Leader" Jamie. Her youth & vigor filled a big spot.
Well I'll stop now cause the worst you can do.
Is leave out a name, whether one or a few.

So next year if it's offered and you've got the time.
Make the trip for yourself; it's far better than this rhyme.

Written by oldbuck
After returning from a trip to
Moody Bible Institute, Chicago, Il.
A Bible school with the aim of
Setting the world on fire for Christ
One student at a time..
Most identities may have been masked or changed see page 100
However: I want to thank Moody for allowing me to use their's.

A Good Friend Moves On....

I'm sitting here now with time on my hands.
Like a silly egg timer with the passing of sand.
I've mixed emotions don't know what I think.
Things can happen quickly, as quick as a wink.

This morning was normal, I showered and shaved.
And promised myself I'd try to behave.
For it's Sunday Morning. We'll soon be in class.
It's good they don't test me for I fear I'd not pass.

I've been in that class, for 30 plus years.
We've had some great times. I suppose shed some tears.
But one things been certain each week that passed by.
My "Teacher" was there. He's a heck of a guy.

He's done it all; He's set up the chairs.
He's been in on decisions and then calmed all our fears.
But this time it seems the moves have been made.
They say when you get lemons you make lemonade.

Well get out the sugar to ease here the sting.
For starting today some changes life brings.
"Teacher" is mobile. He goes where God sends.
He's quick to respond and willing to bend.

It sounds like he's moving to help someone new.
To serve now the seniors, there are more than a few.
Pastors been in there but he's really grown busy.
Balancing his schedule could make the man dizzy.

So as is "Teachers" style he'll strap on that collar.
He won't say a word. No hoop or no holler.
He just sees a job that needs to be done.
If no one steps up, then he'll be the one.

Well this sounds now so sad but calls for celebration.
Now one groups loss is another's elation.
I just want to say before I run out of time.
And close out for now another 'buck' rhyme.

This "Teacher" is special; He's one of a kind.
No matter the need he's not one to mind.
I can here tell you, I'll miss him a lot.
Next Sunday morning when he's not in his spot.

It will cause me to think of all the times he was there.
With most of us here just warming a chair.
Not everyone can teach nor reach out to others.
We can't all be helpmates or be people's brothers.

But we could move chairs, clean chalk boards and such.
Picking up here some slack wouldn't stretch us that much.
So to show our good will, maybe now is the time.
We offer those left that we'll now get in line.

The next time there's a party or something extra to do.
That they should call us and not just a few.
All the class will be there to take up some slack.
To lift now that 'cross' from "new" teachers back.

I'll close with this wish; it's more like a prayer.
If our new teachers need us we'll aim to be there.
So "Teacher", Good Luck. . . No, that's a heathen phrase.
"May God Bless You Richly" as you enter this phase.

As you work with the seniors their thoughts to enrich.
They'll soon grow to love you and hope you won't get the itch.
For each has retired, each one's called it quits.
If you pull that on them, they'll go into great fits. :0)

Written by oldbuck, after learning their "Teacher"
would be leaving for the Seniors group as their teacher / facilitator.

50

RHYME 20

To the readers of this next rhyme:
"As Though to a Timothy."
I must give you a preface to the rhyme or it won't
make any sense. I know what you're thinking,
"It probably won't make any sense anyway". :o)
None the less, read on.

A very wealthy man passed away.
During his lifetime he had donated a large sum to a
private college. In recognition of his philanthropy,
a very large commemorative pewter plate was made
and presented to him.

After his passing, I attended a public portion of his
estate sale. The beautiful plate was there. I couldn't resist it.

We have a fine young man in our church that
attended this same college.

I understand he has a strong public testimony
for Christ and his Faith out on the street.

I thought it might be nice to give the plate to him
since he would have some connection through
the college and would recognize the reason it had
been presented.

I wrote this rhyme as a lesson for him about "intention".

I don't of course know the rich man's intention.
It may have been very generous and well intended.
It may also have had something to do with personal
recognition and ego. I certainly can't say.
I didn't know the fellow at all.

I removed any markings so the original owner was not identifiable.

As you read the rhyme now try to imagine this huge, heavy,
pewter plate in his hand as the young man reads the rhyme.

As Though To A Timothy

To my young brother.
I send this rhyming note.
I may feel as Paul might,
When he sat and wrote.

Those many years ago,
To another bright young man.
That he could glimpse in him,
A powerful leader of a band.

A band of Righteous men
That were to follow at his lead.
His own Christ, to all proclaim
A Saving Faith is all they'd need.

Paul started out his letters
With words about his past belief.
If there had been real evil men
He had ignorantly been their chief.

Then he wrote about the lad
He knew the family well.
And knowing only good of them
Made this story one to tell.

His loving grandma and mother too.
Had always known just what to do.
To raise this boy from youth to man.
Had always kept their God in view.

If this is now about we two.
Then you've been raised up right.
I've been the chief of evil doers
And knowing that is why I write.

For I've this "gift" I give to you,
In hopes, many years from hence.
Serves as a sign of sinful men,
To illustrate a festering stench.

For this now worthless "prize",
Was to me a sign of man's excess.
For if it may have meant a lot for "show"
But a man's own worth it may express.

There may have been in days gone by;
A time of pride and presentation.
Of speeches made and photos flashed.
A time of great "inward" adulation.

But in the end as comes to all,
Its owner too went to his grave,
Death has now been since the fall.
This "Tin", as most, he couldn't save.

There are no pockets in the box,
As surely now as centuries past.
Despite what many want to think.
Only that done for Christ will last.

This "token" may reflect a life exchanged
Day's on earth swapped out for 'this'?
But in the end it was for sale.
For half a buck I shan't resist.

So take this lesson, learn it well,
If a "treasure" you might seek,
When you're facing a temptation.
Make it worthy of Jesus' feet.

For everything we do that lasts
Will add to any crowns we get.
That we might on Judgment Day
At the feet of Jesus then twill set.

Written by oldbuck,
as he thought of what he might pass along to this young man
he's heard such good things about.

It was not his intention to discredit or dishonor the former gift or the "real"
giver he'd never met, nor to imply there is anything inherently evil about
giving charitable gifts to well deserving organizations.

It was merely meant to illustrate how a man's" intentions"
may reveal more of the man, than the gift. . . .
in the end.

I've Been Dreamin' of a "Right" Christmas

I know that Christmas comes
Each year about this time.
But each year it's gettin' harder
To come up with a 'fitting' rhyme.

You see the stores are filled again
With Halloween and Christmas things.
It just don't seem . . . this Santa stuff
Should usher in "The New Born King."

Our culture now as through the years
Has brought us to this awful place.
Where all we do is now "accept"
It's not a part of Christian faith.

For Halloween has always been
A time to beg for Tricks or Treats.
Then Thanksgiving time will come
With all its luscious pies and meats.

So maybe now, let's start a trend
Once and for all we'll see an end.
To all the gifts our Santa's bring
But now instead, our prayers we send.

For God did not rend, His Son so brave
To hang Him there, then to the grave.
That we should teach our kids to crave
But that instead our souls could *Save*.

T'was not for those "infernal" stores.
To jump start next year's sale.
Roasting chestnuts or even smores.
Thinking that . . . makes Christmas pale.

This 'Holly' Season, it's not toys
Or elves or sleigh bells ringing.
Not our families visit from afar
Nor all the gifts they're bringing.

This "Holy "Season was really started
To turn our hearts from every day.
To take a break from all the hustle
To "spend our lives" for more than pay.

So as we make our plans this year
Let's be up-beat, not shed a tear.
Don't mortgage next year's checks
So folks can have the latest gear.

For now's the time to plant New Hope
Renew our hearts, join now as one.
To wish a neighbor, all those we greet
"Peace on Earth" to all who come. .

To this young King from Heaven sent
To save mankind from Hade's pit.
Accept Him now for what He's done
And that will bring an end to it.

For it would make this time worthwhile
If every child, "Christ", could know,
For in their hearts His love would shine
"Peace on Earth" would surely grow.

That is what our Father wants
For that's the essence of His reason.
We should love as we've been loved
"The Reason for the Season".

Written by oldbuck, as he thought of the
excesses and excuses of our culture at this time of year.

We Trim the Christian Tree.

Christmas time brings memories, racing in my head.
However: as I'm growin' old it comes with greater dread.
For shortly after Halloween, before Thanksgiving Day.
Shops will show us "X-mas" wares to make this season pay.

Jolly Santa and his sleigh, Bags of toys and nine reindeer.
Snowmen and candy canes, Mistletoe the young men cheer.
Homemade fudge & ginger cookies, Tasty pies & frosted cakes.
There's one thing sets a part, The Tree that front stage takes.

It's filled with shining lights, sparkling tinsel, thin glass balls.
Tiny elves and Santa's sleigh. Tied on safely against a fall.
Much of this distracts for me, all this "stuff" now on my tree.
I'd rather as my grandkids came, Hints of Christ, for all to see.

As the day now fast approaches and my plastic tree comes out
That has for Oh so many years made "real tree" folk, often pout.
I'll put away our tiny Rudolph with his nose of shining red.
Try to focus at this season on our precious Christ instead.

The Babes mom, Mary

The story here won't be replete without a mention at whose feet.
This young babe will follow in, without sin His life complete.
That day, the young babe's mom heard songs His angels sang,
Who years from now, a loving Son, dying on a cross will hang.

Rough sawn planks

Small rough sawn planks made up the cold hard manger.
While rough sawn beams would bring our Christ, real danger.

A gray donkey

A gray donkey bore His mom to that stable, dark and cold.
To the place where He is born, a humble place, the stories told.
Then on thru Jerusalem's gate. Our King, another donkey rides.
Carried to this fateful stage. A trip from which He did not hide.

Angels

Angel's were a part of this, they sang as Shepherds kept.
Peace on Earth, Good will toward men, as the tiny baby slept.
Near the end the Son of God could ten thousand angels call.
But for our God it was now time for His only Son to fall.

A Lamb

Near that stable a perfect lamb borne on shepherds back,
Was brought along by them to keep it safe from nights attack.
Years hence another place, another Lamb would pay the fee.
On Calvary's Cross would die to save all men. To set them free.

Gifts

Beneath our tree gift packages brightly wrapped, but later torn.
Tell the tale of "Why He's Born". A King with "Crown of Thorns".
On this eve 3 gifts were given for these Magi had felt driven.
To find this tiny babe, to save mankind had now been given.

It's said down through the years, Gold is reserved just for a King.
Frankincense did symbolize a Holiness this King would bring.
The final gift of these, will our hearts through ages bring.
It's been said this precious Myrrh represents His suffering.

For later on another gift this tiny babe would offer.
A gift so freely given, what more can Christ then proffer?
His blood spilled, a life would end, beaten, bruised, and torn.
This King of Kings & Lord of Lords, for all men's sins had borne.

A Tiny Stable Cave

There was no room, but offered humble stables cave.
Then as fate, for His grave another stranger gave.
A fitting place our Savior, could his bloodied head now lay,
If only there for then a three day stay.

Strips of Cloth

Clean swaddling clothes. And what of these?
To wrap the babe from nights cool breeze.
To shield His gentle skin, so tender, young, and soft,
From all the scratchy harshness of a lowly cattle trough.

But at His grave revealed at mornings light.
Where He had lay, and folded there just right.
Those burial cloths that offered fragrance flood.
As now those cloths are stained with blood.

A star

Atop our tree, a star will shine as one Wise men followed there.
To point the way to this new babe, born to die it don't seem fair.
It was in evening's darkness the lovely star shone bright.
But in the day of this Kings death the day was turned to night.

Just as sure as that star shone believers know we're not alone.
Our Christ lives and waits for us to share in His eternal home.
As we approach this busy time, some things no longer pleasin'.
Much to do, much to spend. Yer runnin' for no good reason.

Step back and think it through. Is this Christ's plan for you?
When He was born in Bethlehem. For this lost world to view?
If you're trapped and wearin' thin, for no rhyme nor reason.
Remember now and years to come,

The Reason for the Season.

Written by oldbuck, in
preparation for the Christmas Rush
and all that brings to our homes.

If some Christmas season you find yourself "trimming" your tree with all the regular "stuff". You might find one of the items above to place on the tree to represent to all that would see it, the story you have just read and
The Reason For The Season.
May He Bless you in a special way if you do.

I'd be remiss if I didn't mention here, something I read just today.
Rachel Stephenson in her blog "Finding the Holy in a Mundane World"
She mentions a 4th Gift given. She described it as "The Gift of Worship".
To learn more details, give her site a visit.

I've Heard
The Voice of Angels

On the eve of Jesus birth
A band of angels came to earth.
To share with us our Saviors birth
To tell us of our "Kings" great worth.

To lowly shepherds, lambs & ewes
A choir of angels shared the news.
It was for all a special night
Filled with awe but not with fright.

Well in my life I've sometimes thought
What memory that sound might wrought?
Well just last night would be my turn
For yet that eve I too would learn.

The sound of angels standing near
Each one wanting to catch my ear.
Each hand filled with strength and care
Each one willing help to share.

For I was sick, too sick to rise
At times too sick to open eyes.
This band of angels by my side
Were there to offer a helping ride.

Each one knew what they must do
Well trained hands so deftly flew.
I knew at once I'd be O.K.
Each one assured by what they'd say.

The last I remember before my ride
Maintenance would "Get the Tide."
My "full time" angel drove the hack
As I sat comfortably leaning back.

We've just arrived. More help is near
Silly me I shouldn't fear.
A nurse had said she'd send with care
A notice that we'd soon be there.

~ ~ ~ ~

This side note: A tale will tell
Mom always said: "What if you fell?
And to a doctor's care would rush
Holey "undies" would make you blush. "

Will it's a fact; I'll tell it here
My "undies" are brand new this year.
Daughter's family, fixed dad up
Far better than an ugly tie or silly coffee cup.

~ ~ ~ ~

Two male angels stripped me down
Got me in a backless gown.
One reassured me "All was well"
It was good to lose that smell.

There was now on each weakened arm
Folks with needles but meant no harm.
One with meds . . . fluids to provide
One to check "what's goin' on inside."

There's an EKG & chest x-rays
I hope for some insurance pays.
They want to know for certain here
All the fault is in my ear.

I'd be remiss if I didn't mention
The Doc that got my full attention.
He's from the South 'twas plain to tell
He was from Nashville & sang as well.

God had sent him there that eve
For me. . . . . . to fill a special need.
For I'm no good round strangers pokin'
But he was cool and filled with jokin'.

To cap the list of angels seen
Our Pastor Jay came onto the scene
As Doc then shared his special "Glory"
When Christ came into his life's story.

All were there to hear the news
In spite of others often views.
All the tests confirmed at last
I'll be as "NORMAL" as in the past.

I'll take my pills and hope for best
I aim to never be the pest.
For this great band of angels present
Another time mayn't be so pleasant.

But this I take from what was done

The Voice of Angels
Is a Comforting One.

Written by oldbuck,
After a bout with "Vertigo" that started
at church as he waited for the evening service to begin.
I raised quite a fuss and made quite a mess. 8^)
We have several trained medical folk that attend our church that are always
quick to respond to any medical emergency there.

My Inner Ego or The Great "I am"

I oft have tiny voices whispering in my head.
At times I must admit. I'm not sure just what they said.
Cause sometimes when I'm thinkin' things that they suggest,
Can't be the thing to do. Can't be for me the best.

I've thought the problem over and choose to do the right.
But then I do the other with troubles in plain sight.
Later then it's crystal clear; Pride over rides my greatest fears.
Then I find my very life is drenching wet with tears.

My ego takes control of me then oft directs my way.
Even though I think I should I seldom get my say.
What can an old man do? He's set his course in life.
Even when he knows for sure his actions bring great strife.

I think it's all just in my head, that's where those voices live.
If they were coming from my heart, I might have more to give.
To overcome my lifelong trends they say you can't just shed.
You have to find a better way to spend that time instead.

For trying hard to "give it up" they say just leaves a void.
You can't live without a heart like a modern day android.
Where on earth can I now turn? To find this strength & hope.
Some folks look inside themselves but for me, I'd be a dope.

I've done that and came up short; it's where the troubles started.
I must look for something new if from "troubles" to be parted.
"Christ above, The only Way." I've heard from some I trust,
He's filled with love and grace. He waits to share it now or bust.

Could I find this "Loving God"? Some call "The Holy Ghost."
He's right here and wanting, to work with you, to be your host.
The Bible says: "Just turn from sin a full one hundred eighty.
But with my past it scares me, is sounding pretty "weighty."

The promise is: "He's always there "To help in time of need.
No matter what the problem, be it gossip, lust, or greed.
I'll ask Him now to fill my heart, my life to over flowing.
From now and ever after I'll know where I am going.

I'll take my cross; now happily, follow Him to Heaven's door.
To live with Him eternally, that means: For ever more.

Written by oldbuck, after hearing
a wonderful sermon about denying self
and serving Him.

Matthew 16: 24-26

This Hand Cross

This cross is just a piece of wood,
Of its self it has no power.
But the Great "I AM" it represents,
Stands as a mighty tower.

Use it to remind yourself,
He loves you, Oh so much.
He has even died for you,
It's something you can touch.

He's alive and loves you still,
No matter what you've done.
And when He comes again,
You can be His number one.

But till that awesome Day,
The Comforter we share.
Now cast on Him your burdens,
You'll find He answers prayer.

Use this Cross to prompt you,
To be thankful day by day.
To always now remember,
How His blessings come your way.

Use it as an anchor point,
Surrender now your will.
Jesus Christ is waiting near,
Your heart He wants to fill.

For where else would a person go,
With life's problems large or small.
But to The Lord now of your life,
Who will solve them once for all.

Written by oldbuck, at the request
of a friend that makes beautiful, wooden Hand Crosses.

In Recognition of Your Absence.

I don't keep any written records
I have no lengthy made up list.
Of those that may be present here
Or who today may have missed.

But my eyes are quickly drawn
To any vacant seats or pews.
Then I try to place a name
For your absence now is news.

It's not because I need to know
Things come up in every life.
A thoughtful hubby stayed at home
With sick children or his wife.

However: I've said this oft before
Your absence I can't ignore.
Because I care about your strife
But don't aim to be a snoopy bore.

Through the years as I've been gone
Some reasons shan't be shared.
But was always nice to hear a voice
Next Sunday, say:"They cared".

So take this silly rhyme
For why it's being shared.
My simple way of saying
"To let you know I cared".

Written by oldbuck
As he thought of those that might
be missing next Sunday.

RHYME 27

It's Good to See You at Inner Mission

It's good to see you.
We're glad you've come today.
I'd like to help you feel at home.
I'm "oldbuck"; some just call me "hay".

Welcome to Inner –Mission
A time that we can stand and chat
That time each week we share a cup.
Or munch a treat to break our fast.

I don't know how long you've come
For many years or just brand new.
I pray we'll meet again real soon
Our acquaintance to renew.

I've written many other rhymes
That oft have gone un - read.
You were kind and turned to here
I hope, won't dread it now instead.

I trust before we parted ways
I thought to get you name.
I seldom will remember them
But want to ask it all the same.

The next time that we meet
Please remind me who you are.
I often will remember faces
Guessing names. . . . I'm off too far.

So that is all I have today
A handshake and a grin.
I hope this time of fellowship
Will bring us "face to face" again.

oldbuck

Written by oldbuck, as something to leave
with new folks he would meet at Inner Mission. A half hour "meet & greet"
time between Sunday school & Church.

I've found it helpful as I meet new people if I can have something
tangible to leave with them. It need not be a rhyme but some little
"thing" that helps cement, for both of us, our short moments together.

The following is something that I often use "out & about".
It's a fun way to break the ice with new folk.
I try to carry a couple copies in my bill fold.
Maybe this will prompt your thinking about "tools" you could use as you
"travel this sod", bumping into new folks, nearly every day.
****
Hello: My name is "oldbuck"
I love to meet new people.
It's almost a curse on me.
I got it from my granddad.
He always felt a stranger,
Was just a friend he'd never met.

My problem is I struggle to remember names.
I meet someone and try to associate the name
with a common item. However:
that doesn't work as well as it used to.

An example: I recently met a man named Remington.
I associated that with fire arms.
Today if I met him I would struggle to know
if his name were "Smith or Wesson". :o)

RHYME 28

He Deserves a Moment of Our Time.

On the cross He hung & bled.
When taken down . . . He was dead.
But in the grave He would not stay
O'er even death, He'd have His sway.

Now He sits at God's right hand
Through Spirit's power rules our land.
He died for sinners. . . you and me
For in the end.. . . Judgment will be.

But there's a thing that you must do.
If in "The End "this works for you.
Accept Him now o'er sin & strife
Then you may have eternal life.

Then as a token of your thanks
As you pause for hot beef shanks.
You might say some words of Grace.
Before you stuff your pudgy face.

Written by oldbuck
After he had seen a young family, say
a short blessing together in a busy
eating place. It didn't take long,
but I'm sure the Lord was smiling.

I've often heard folks say: "They just don't know yet how to pray".
I'm of the mind that if you bowed your head and said:
Here's the bread and here's the meat.
Thank you God for these great eats.
Amen
I believe: He knows your true intention.
Isn't so concerned, about your own rendition.

A Season of No Reason

Thanksgiving turkey's in the oven
The silver's spit and polished.
The fact that it's a special day
Is clearly now acknowledged.

I passed around some flyers
To my neighbors, sent email.
I want each to be reminded
Why we gather without fail.

So now my mind looks ahead
It's the dawn of coming "Season".
You know, the one we shop & spend
For "So many silly reasons".

You think the local merchant's
Greed had planned it all.
But later added "extra" days
To draw you to their Mall.

For now the frosty pumpkin's
Still on our front stoop.
A reminder of winter's coming
Wet snow that we can scoop.

You've see them in the paper
Colored ads start in high gear.
You could always tell from that
Old Santa's time was near.

But that was weeks ago
That Magic day is still far off.
The re-cycle guy is weighted down
To "Merry Christmas" he might scoff.

I'll go into hiding now
This is my season's habit.
When I even hear those words
I run like a scared rabbit.

But don't let me spoil your fun
You have lots of stuff to do.
Find those gifts and wrap'em
Then hide them out of view.

Make extensive family party plans
Stock-up now your "bulging" pantries.
Frost sheets of "Sugar" cookies
For all our Santa's "Grand entries".

For many, these are special days
They look forward all year long.
But with it all, there is great stress
To me that seems all wrong.

It should be a time, Of Peace On Earth
Great Joy should fill the air.
But instead the credit charges
Have us pulling out our hair.

We should do ourselves a favor
Keep a smile to spread around.
"Noel" sung by Caroler's voices
Be the holiday's loudest sound.

Might we pledge to share our time
As the gift we give each other.
Spend Holiday cash on stuff to give
To some starving kids and mother.

We'd all be happier in the end
Our Lord, His hope, we'd found.
If all this season what He'd hear
His Gospel Story spread around.

For God has always been
He wanted man to share His life.
He fashioned us in his own image
Since young Adam and his wife.

But it wasn't long before a sin
Had entered man's cold heart.
God would send His only Son
In a manger, got his humble start.

Many of you will know the rest
Many more have never heard.
So in the weeks ahead my friends
Let's get out and share His Word.

For it's a story of a Gift
Most precious gift of all.
He has provided Eternal Life
Just now, on His Name Call.

This year could be "a best" for you
If something you say may spark.
If you might be the one He'll use
To reach some lost soul's heart.

So let's make Christmas time
As was planned so many years ago.
Bring out the best in each of us
As Christ's love to all we show.

This will bring again for all
A Reason for the Season.

Written by oldbuck
As he thought ahead to the weeks to come
Feeling it may have become a season of no reason.

I realize this is the 3rd or 4th Christmas Season rhyme.
I'm also aware the story line is always about the same.
But it's difficult to improve or change much,
The Beginning of: The Greatest Story Ever Told.
Christ's birth, life, death and Resurrection
for all of mankind that might accept it.
That includes His plan for "you".
8^)

A Coat of Many Colors,
Just the Start of Something Great.

A long, long time ago, in a land way far away.
There was a large family, all boys by the way.
This father had 12 son's by the time this tales done.
Only one had "His" Spirit, God shows us which one.

But I'm going too fast, this story to share.
However: It's exciting, God's love & great care.
Will abide with this one through good times and sad.
But not matter the status the boy never turns bad.

It started with a coat, one the father had made for son.
For by Joseph's very actions his father's heart he had won.
He was obedient and kind to his friends and 11 brothers.
Only one ends a full brother, they share the same mother.

Will his dad couldn't help it, He loved this young lad.
So he made a great coat, a special gift from the dad.
It was a coat like no other, Bright colors and fine trim.
Older brothers were upset, when dad gave it to "him".

Well our story continues, the ten older lads.
Were sent to the pastures to watch sheep for old dad.
Some time had now passed, Father filled up with care.
He'd send out young Joseph a report to then share.

There were already ill feelings Twixt Joseph and the others.
They really didn't feel at all like 'true' brothers.
You see Joseph had 2 dreams he was able to understand.
He shared them with everyone, these dreams split the band.

For he stated the truth of the dreams he had seen.
That he would be honored or so it would seem.
So now with that background you may well understand.
The ten might take advantage of the situation now at hand.

One felt they should kill him, put an end to his pride.
But still there's the problem of how do you hide.
This sudden disappearance of a young healthy boy.
It's not just the same as losing a small toy.

Someone spotted a deep pit, an empty well or so it seems.
They'd throw him there to die but his God would intervene.
Along came a caravan of traders, rough and mean.
They'd sell him for some silver. Never again by them be seen.

So that is what they did. They got some twenty "bucks".
Maybe watched as he rode off, they were tickled with their luck.
It was only Reuben the oldest, planned to save him from the pit.
But he was away in a pasture, when he returned he had a fit.

The other brothers explained they were sparing Joseph's life.
As well as remove this source of constant trouble and ill strife.
They cut Joseph's coat in shreds and killed a young goat.
They'd tell the curious dad that's his blood on colored coat.

Our story turns back to this lad who's taken to foreign lands.
Finds himself now being sold, into a wealthy Potiphar's hand.
It wasn't long before Potiphar would see this "slave" was good.
Soon he placed him at the top. Our God's young Joseph stood.

If our story ended there, it seems things turned out right.
But the devil won't give up without some evil fight.
It seems here Satan set a plan, Potiphar's wife to set her spark.
To get this handsome man off in a room and in the dark.

Joseph, a chosen one of God's. Good & righteous & not inclined.
To let temptation win him over or his conscience now go blind.
How could he do it, such a very bad thing?
For this passionate lady wore the ring of his "king".

After many tries the wife grew mean, felt rebuffed by this fine lad.
She lied to Potiphar about events which then made him mad.
Joseph finds himself in prison unjustly accused and sent.
But to be an honorable prisoner his mind was rightly bent.

It wouldn't be too long the jailer saw this winner.
He recognized this fellow was no-where near a sinner.
He placed Joseph then in charge over all the other inmates.
Here is just another time; God controls this young man's fate.

Then on God's own schedule, Great Pharaoh had two dreams.
He asked his magician's. "What can they both mean?"
They stammered and stuttered really had not a notion.
But Pharaoh's cup bearer heard all the commotion.

He had to come clean for he had been lax.
He had forgotten a promise to share the hard facts.
Of how Jacob had read a dream that he'd had.
That he'd be set free no longer viewed as bad.

He'd made the promise to remember Jacob's skill.
Sharing with Pharaoh. His dreams to fulfill.
Pharaoh sent for Jacob. They got him cleaned up.
Then brought him in to get those dreams tallied up.

Pharaoh demanded the truth. Jacob said "he couldn't do it".
But his God surely could. . . . He soon would get right too it.
It wasn't good news. Seven years of great plenty.
Then seven years of dire want. For food, there just isn't any.

God then had commanded: Pharaoh find a wise & honest man.
To rule all Egypt's land, to set up a firm, life savings plan.
Pharaoh judged no one else could interpret those 2 dreams.
Jacob now would rule all of Egypt so it seems.

Pharaoh gave him his ring that would tell everyone.
The wearer of this was Pharaoh's "number 1".
Well there's more to this story but we've gone on long enough.
We'll start fresh and new once we've studied more stuff.

Written by oldbuck
As another attempt at a children's
Bible Study rhyme.

He Promises Blessings,
If We "Do What Jesus Did".

This is my third rhyme
From out of His Good Book.
There are dozens more
Some time just take a look.

But now . . right here . . today
Let's take our own quick peek.
To see now the direction
That this great story seeks.

Jesus and His new found twelve
Had gone up, what seemed, a quiet hill.
To be alone, to share with them
This hill, they thought, might fit the bill.

He wanted here to teach them
To follow close His lead.
So when at last He'd gone away
New Believers, they could feed.

As he started, then to share
A crowd formed and closely followed.
For some how they had known
This ground would be now hallowed.

For Christ would here today
Present to all their hearts.
The basic Truths of life
The best ways now to start.

Blessed are the poor in spirit.
He was speaking out against our pride.
For theirs is the kingdom of heaven
But for no one a free ride.

For as we come to Him.
It's a living attitude thing.
For what we must daily do
Is His true humility bring.

Blessed are they that mourn
Those words sounded strange
For they shall be comforted
Something Christ would pre-arrange.

For when he left us here
To hold down now "the fort".
He provided us "The Comforter"
Which offers "real" support.

Blessed are the meek
Here he don't mean chickens.
Meek shall inherit the earth
But it won't be easy pickin's.

For the devil is right beside you
He wants to steal your heart.
So be kind and gentle always
Hold your temper just for starts.

Blessed are they that hunger
Who thirst for righteousness.
For they shall all be filled
Don't describe a banquet fest.

But rather now instead
Our Lord, here may just mean.
If your heart is in the right place
Your thoughts toward Him will lean.

Blessed are they
Who show mercy to others.
Be good to them always
As if they're Sisters and Brothers.

For the promise that we see
"Mercy shown to them".
Following this "Golden Rule"
Will reward and not condemn.

Blessed are they
Who have a pure heart.
For they shall see God
When from earth they depart.

Blessed are they always
That make peace among man.
For they shall be called
Children of the great "I AM."

Blessed are they who are persecuted
For the sake of righteousness.
For as they near the end of life
They'll have little to confess.

When they stand at the gate
To their "Kingdom of Heaven".
They won't have to trust a lottery
To any numbers . . like a 3 or 7.

So in these words our Lord put out
We see what a "Christian" does.
He showed us all just how to pray
What enemies did, what friendship was.

He gave his word these blessing come
To those of faith who take a stand.
Don't in this life give to temptation
Or join the devil and his demons band.

He ends it now with a rock and loose sand.
Both as spots to build a home.
He on the solid rock shall stand
While sand won't leave your home alone.

The secret is: "Trust and obey"
Don't from His ways, a little stray
You'll be happy here in Jesus
Trusting in Him, all the way.

Written by oldbuck
In his third attempt at bringing out
Bible Truth with a rhyme. This was difficult to write
because he feared it may have disrupted
the Inerrancy of the Scriptures
in trying to make it all rhyme.
An apology to "Him" for that.

Until we meet again.

Here in this brass urn
Are just ashes and bone.
But I've added my prayers
He'll not go alone.

I fear my prayers are now ignored
As he nears the "Golden" gate.
If he's made no prior decision
I suspect it's far too late.

But I feel I should say them
He was not a "bad" guy.
I certainly wouldn't want him
For all eternity to fry.

In the years that I knew him
As a friend. . . . more a chum.
He was seldom then lazy
Nor lived as a bum.

He loved to bring smiles
On folks sad or sullen faces.
Often voicing weird comments
In the oddest of places.

There's one thing I know
Has now given relief.
When we spoke of Jesus
He oft shared his "Belief."

For that's all that matters
To then get inside.
For it is only Believers
With "Him" will reside.

So if as you read this
You've given it thought.
And ask if your "goodness"
A "mansion" has bought.

You've read it here now
But it's always been so.
Without Faith in Jesus
It's to hell you must go.

But "You" still have time
Set your pride aside.
Tell Jesus you trust Him
Want to be now His "bride".

Written by oldbuck
As he thought of friends who've gone on ahead.
How many had he failed to tell because it
might have affected their relationship.
* * * * * * * * * * *

I've handed out a few copies of it, with this request.
If they attend my funeral, I would like them to read this.
I've made my family agree, there will be a good luncheon.

oldbuck

WHEN BAD STUFF HAPPENS

It's hard here to deny.
We often scream out, Oh My God.
I can't understand . . . . Why?

Well I may have an answer
I keep back in my mind.
At times of great trouble
When answers I can't find.

God has a vantage point
Though He needs no outside help.
He sees the total picture
Even hears your mournful "yelp".

But He's long since, made a plan
For your life and for mine.
He can take our daily hardships
Make them work out really fine.

That isn't here to say
It will be all milk and honey
Or as you travel on your route
You'll end with lots of money.

No. . the plan that He has drawn
Is filled with great life tests.
In the midst, it's hard to keep in mind
The Father does know best.

But if you're praying daily
Kneeling often at His feet.
You'll find it comes much easier
The next time that you meet.

Old Satan, the Great tempter
That "Snake" with world's appeal.
When over your left shoulder
He makes you some big deal.

A promise of an easy street
Of a safe and comfy passage.
If it sounds way too good
You best grab your coat & baggage.

You will flee from that spot
As naturally as can be.
For Bible truths will guide you
Help you more clearly see.

When something "earthly" happens
He'll be there at your side.
As that's where you've been spending
Oft your days to there reside.

For when Christ left this place
His promise made to us.
He'd send "His own" a comforter
For when times are but a bust.

A helpmate filled with powers
Far beyond what we could find.
Anything we would ask
Or might ever come to mind.

He's mercifully promised
Gifts from His Holy Spirit.
He called them simply "fruits"
A part of Salvations merit.

So if you find a Loving spirit
Shows itself now in your life.
Or a feeling of abundant Joy
In the midst of a great strife.

If you have Peace or Patience
Amidst a world that has gone wild.
Self-Control, even Kindness and/or
Gentleness, when others are less mild.

Then when your life is filled
With a Faithfulness that's free.
You'll plainly see with Goodness
How great this life can be.

But that's not the end
Of His story now we tell.
For it started during times
With things going not so well.

Maybe here's the best part
For the answer to our "Why."
Has been promised . . . but for later
As for now we'll just stand by.

So remember as a "Chosen One"
With Christ, full in your heart.
Those days filled with troubles
Needn't be a crippling part.

Keep speaking of Him daily
Share the very best you can.
Remembering how Our Father
Works His "Masterful" plan.

Written by oldbuck, after hearing about a young man,
who strived daily to do the Lord's work,
snuffed out in a moment by a careless driver.

We missed ya, Classmate.

Please forgive this silly rhyme
But we're just trying to touch base.
Because today in Sunday school
We didn't see your smiling face.

No one can always be there
Stuff oft times makes that so.
But if we don't recognize the void
How can our family closer grow.

Of course it isn't just for numbers
It's to show we really care.
Want you to surely know
We missed you in your chair.

For each of us brings something new
Whether you speak or pray or smile.
All those little things you do
Let us know you'd go the mile.

If we were having problems
We would find your help not lacking.
So if this would find you in a snag
We shan't wait to offer backing.

So we'll close now with this wish
For you and yours the very best.
And hope to see you come next Sunday
Sitting there with all the rest.

Written by oldbuck, to mail to
those we miss in Adult Bible Class.

A Thanksgiving Day Reminder

Oct. 3rd 1789, President Washington
Made a Proclamation.
That all American's everywhere
<u>All across our glorious nation.</u>
Should set a special day aside
To spend eating and in prayer.
To thank our Gracious God
<u>For the blessings we now share.</u>
It's not about a Roasted Turkey
Sweet-taters or green beans.
It's about all His blessings
<u>What today that really means.</u>
He was there when we were starting
He's been with us through fierce wars.
Has shown us His great mercy
<u>Fought at home or foreign shores.</u>
So with His help, we've prospered
Through His wisdom we have learned.
As nations watched our progress
<u>A place of leadership we have earned.</u>
So on this special day we share
Let us be mindful whence it came.
Keep our hearts and minds on Him
<u>For it may not always be the same.</u>
So with that solemn thought
I will add this festive cheer.
Spend now the day enjoying it
With loved ones near and dear.

Written by oldbuck, to pass around the neighborhood to remind each
of us, the significance of the day. Maybe some will ask a child or
grandchild to read it before the meal as a conversation starter.

We Prepare for a Downpour
The Rains of Revival

This Encounter With God
Will Soak You With Joy.

If you're feeling "off"
Your "spirit" life's stale.
Prepare for a Downpour
It's not just a tale.

You can have the power
Of a "battery fired-up" bunny.
You might now laugh
But it's really not funny.

A fresh surge of energy
To labor for the King.
It comes from the Spirit
It's a life-changing thing.

God is not reluctant
He's ready right now.
It's repentance He's after
Just at his feet bow.

Joy is renewed
By choices you make.
And in direct response
To actions you take.

It's refilling you need
But first must make room.
Flush out devil's sin
Regrets, fear, and gloom.

"Return to the Lord".
Let us press on to know him.
He will come to us like rain
Filling "spirit" to the brim.

It you want the Holy Spirit
To on your life rain.
You now must make certain
Of your life, He has reign.

Written by oldbuck,
after piecing together the last 8-10 wks
of Adult Bible Class.

When Life Doesn't Seem Fair.

Since my dog's life expired, here's been my silent wish.
Will she be there in heaven? I've hoped as I pondered this,

Our pets so oft' become like a part of the family.
We'd generally expect them; it's not a strange anomaly.

There are two sides of a story as is so often the case.
When we hinge our dreams without hard facts to base.

I've read some good blogs that sound really swell,
But like much on the internet it's often . . . so hard to tell.

One older lady wrote in her blog, she doesn't offer sound proof.
But agrees with many believers, God's eternal love is no spoof.

Even some old preachers with years of good sense.
Won't offer up scriptures to restrict pets at the fence.

If God's allows all creatures to endure suffering and death.
Why shouldn't they receive His loving . . . eternal breathe.

Now that would seem fair. all our funny, faithful pets.
All living happily together in bright, solid 'gold' nests.

Lions & Lambs, various dogs & house cats.
Turtles & goldfish, tiny mice & big white rats.

But wait just a bit, who said Heaven is fair.
Look at the foul mixture of sinners He'd spare.

If Hitler had but spoken a sincere bit of prayer.
Repented of his ghastly sins. God's heaven he'd share.

What about you & me? Aren't we "one of those" kind?
That if' 'they' peeled us back are we more that a rind?

Christ always insisted; there's none, no not one.
That would "deserve" to pass but for God's sinless Son.

So as I linger longer on this "well" deep issue.
I'll be satisfied with this. I won't need any tissue.

For when I reach that gate, pain and grief left behind.
If I only see Jesus, how could anyone mind?

Written by oldbuck,
as he thought about Fairness,
Heaven, Pets and God's love.

* * * * * * * * * * * * * * *

A thought to ponder from the author:

When God creates the New Heaven & New Earth.
Wouldn't the New Eden be filled with the animals God said were "Good"?
The animals He put there originally for the pleasure of man.
It sounds like: Man's pets. :o)

You pray, While Jesus Seeks

Each morning as I peek out
Our mail box, there to see.
I'm watching for the postman.
What he might bring for me.

When I see him coming
Stopping just across the street.
I know in just a moment
My "deliverer" I will meet.

Today is no exception
I go rushing out to find.
To see who knows my name
Will share what's on their mind.

I find there's something special
A lengthy letter from a friend.
He always has something timely
As though he knows just where I am.

It's about God's daily practice
Of looking out for all of us.
What we can do to help the lost
Without raising now a fuss.

He includes a handy message
About 'saving our lost friends".
How folks often work and worry
It's a contagious & growing trend.

We get bent all out of shape
We worry they won't find.
Or they might somehow grow weary
Heaven might "slip their mind".

He quoted from Luke 19, verse 10.
Christ came to search out & save the lost.
We often think that we can save
But always find. . . . His Spirit is the boss.

Ezekiel 34:11 So says the Lord God:
"God himself will search for the Lost sheep"
The lost's "seeking" is from the Spirit
All "God's Chosen" hearts are His to keep.

So what's my part, what could I do
For my lost friends heart to sway.
That they may find "Salvation Free"
In God's Heaven . . . . forever stay.

Pray to the Holy Spirit
Bringing often your friend's name.
The Spirit opens hearts
When it happens . . . not always the same.

But another verse was offered
To encourage us as we start.
Luke 18:1, Jesus taught, *We should*
Always keep praying, never losing heart.

I found those words uplifting
They've given me new hope.
As I worry about lost friends
I won't feel such a helpless dope.

Written by oldbuck
After receiving an encouraging letter from a friend.

In The End. . . . The Answer

What can this old guy do?
Rhyming words runnin' in my head.
There when I get up
Even worse when I'm in bed.

Someone may have said:
"Just write them down to share."
But when I spent the time
No one seemed at all to care.

Is it a curse or something worse
This gnawing, creepy, cross I bear.
Or is there yet some message
Hidden deep inside I'm led to share.

The only "message" worth repeating
Has been written long ago.
For God's own story of His plan.
In the Bible, we read its flow.

How could a silly rhymer
Bring a special meaning
To anything so sacred
It doesn't need repeating.

I guess it's back to staring down
The one eyed monsters sway.
That enters hearts through idle minds
Then leads so many folks astray.

But: What will be my answer?
When my life is finally o'er?
What will I say standing there?
What was my "gift" spent for?

So I'll just share it now
What God's promise means to me.
My trust in 'Christ' will get me in
For His life was given Free.

There will be things
I should have done.
None matter, not at all
For Trusting Him's the only one.

A simple prayer now uttered
That simple act of "turning round"
Laying bare your stubborn heart
Forever now on hallowed ground.

If this seems far too easy
There is something you should know.
It's not all roses you receive
He'll expect you now to grow.

Some will take offense
You'll be burdened, Christ to share.
But remember this one thing
The results are not your care.

For He's sent His Holy Spirit
To stand along beside.
You can't do the saving
He'll decide where they reside.

So jump down off your high horse
Repent today, and be set free.
The angels will rejoice above
And remember: There's no fee.

Written by oldbuck, one evening
after spending a rather pensive day.

If you've actually read this far, Thank you. I realize I'm no poet
but have felt lead to write these little rhymes and dozens more
over a period of about 8 years.
I've handed out dozens, yes maybe even hundreds of copies
of these 39 rhymes and many more.
I felt I had pretty much worn out my local audience and wanted
to give others an opportunity. 8^)
Thanks again for taking a chance on this book.
I trust it had some good moments mixed in with the others.

A Special Note of Thanks

It just wouldn't be right if I didn't mention Billy Graham and BGEA.

He and his organization have been a constant source of Christian inspiration to me for over 50 years.

Reading their magazine, watching his "Crusade" messages on T.V. and all the other Gospel information they provide, has been like having another "church" supporting me in my Walk.

Thank you Billy Graham, your family, and the entire organization for all you have done for me and countless millions of others around the world.

* *

I would also like to acknowledge some of the wonderful speakers we heard while at Moody Bible Institute.

Crawford Loritts, Strength for the Journey.
David Kinnaman & Gabe Lyons, The unchristian generation.
Gary Haugen, We are the Plan.
Francis Chan, Crazy Love, Abounding in Love for One Another.
Charles Colson, A Perfect Storm
Erwin Lutzer, The Battle for the Gospel: False Prophets.

I'm sorry I didn't take better notes and couldn't remember their specific order or message presented. All were great.

* * * * * * * * * * * * * * * * * * *

I don't view this as "The End" but rather just the beginning.

44038426R00061

Made in the USA
Charleston, SC
12 July 2015